The Voyage of Odysseus

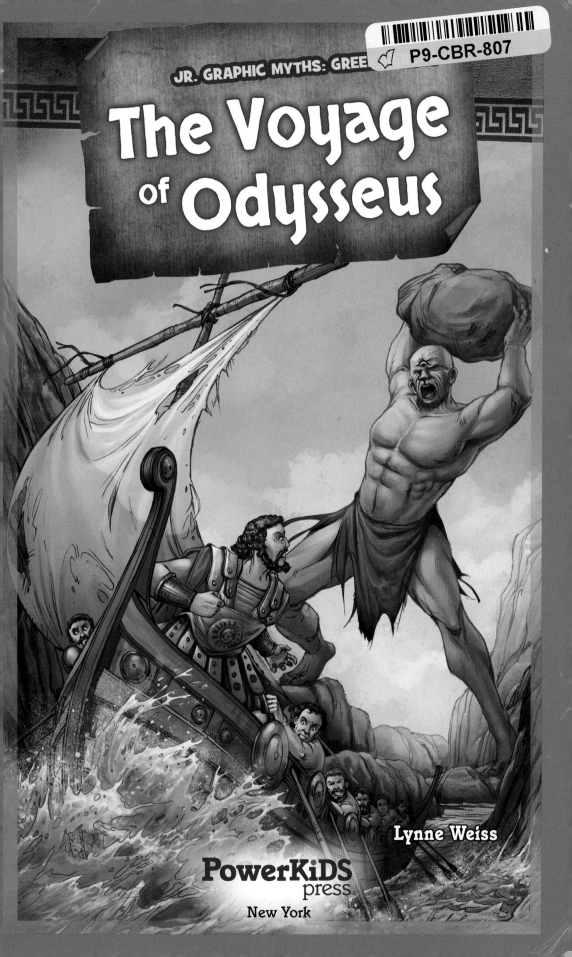

Lynne Weiss

PowerKiDS
press

New York

Published in 2014 by The Rosen Publishing Group, Inc.
29 East 21st Street, New York, NY 10010

First Edition

Editor: Joanne Randolph
Book Design: Contentra Technologies
Illustrations: Contentra Technologies

Library of Congress Cataloging-in-Publication Data

Weiss, Lynne, 1952–
 The voyage of Odysseus / by Lynne Weiss. — First Edition.
    pages cm. — (Jr. graphic myths: Greek heroes)
 Includes index.
 ISBN 978-1-4777-6244-8 (library) — ISBN 978-1-4777-6245-5 (pbk.) —
ISBN 978-1-4777-6246-2 (6-pack)
 1. Odysseus (Greek mythology)—Juvenile literature. 2. Homer. Odyssey—
Juvenile literature. I. Title.
 BL820.O3W45 2014
 883'.01—dc23
                                        2013026123

Manufactured in the United States of America
CPSIA Compliance Information: Batch #W14PK1: For Further Information contact Rosen Publishing, New York,
New York at 1-800-237-9932

Contents

Introduction

Greek mythology is filled with stories of epic battles, **heroes**, monsters, and hardships endured by **mortals**. In this myth, Odysseus, the hero of the Trojan War, sails toward home with his crew of 500 men when the war is over. The voyage is filled with danger. Will the men who survived the long, hard Trojan War survive the terrible journey home?

Main Characters

 Odysseus King of Ithaca, hero of the Trojan War.

 Penelope Wife of Odysseus, queen of Ithaca.

 Telemachus Son of Penelope and Odysseus.

 Polyphemus One-eyed giant and son of Poseidon.

 Circe Goddess who was known for her **transformative** potions and magic.

 Calypso Goddess who is portrayed as a sea **nymph**.

The Voyage of Odysseus

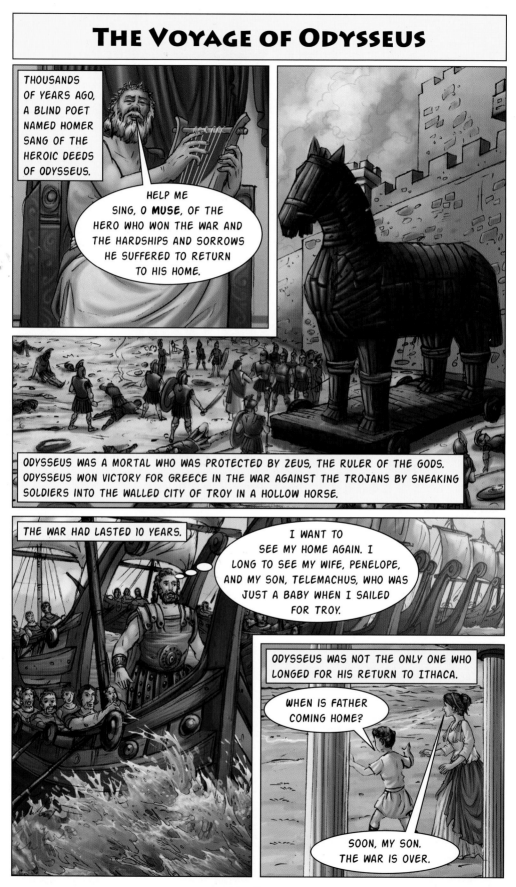

THOUSANDS OF YEARS AGO, A BLIND POET NAMED HOMER SANG OF THE HEROIC DEEDS OF ODYSSEUS.

HELP ME SING, O **MUSE**, OF THE HERO WHO WON THE WAR AND THE HARDSHIPS AND SORROWS HE SUFFERED TO RETURN TO HIS HOME.

ODYSSEUS WAS A MORTAL WHO WAS PROTECTED BY ZEUS, THE RULER OF THE GODS. ODYSSEUS WON VICTORY FOR GREECE IN THE WAR AGAINST THE TROJANS BY SNEAKING SOLDIERS INTO THE WALLED CITY OF TROY IN A HOLLOW HORSE.

THE WAR HAD LASTED 10 YEARS.

I WANT TO SEE MY HOME AGAIN. I LONG TO SEE MY WIFE, PENELOPE, AND MY SON, TELEMACHUS, WHO WAS JUST A BABY WHEN I SAILED FOR TROY.

ODYSSEUS WAS NOT THE ONLY ONE WHO LONGED FOR HIS RETURN TO ITHACA.

WHEN IS FATHER COMING HOME?

SOON, MY SON. THE WAR IS OVER.

ODYSSEUS SAILED FOR TROY WITH 12 SHIPS FULL OF GREEK SOLDIERS. THEY CAME FROM ODYSSEUS'S HOME ON THE ISLAND OF ITHACA AND FROM THE SURROUNDING ISLANDS. NOW ODYSSEUS GATHERED HIS SHIPS AND HIS MEN, AND THEY SET SAIL FOR HOME.

GETTING HOME WAS HARDER THAN ODYSSEUS EXPECTED, THOUGH. A TERRIBLE STORM BLEW HIS SHIPS OFF COURSE.

THE SHIPS CAME TO A BEAUTIFUL ISLAND. A SMALL GROUP OF SAILORS SET OFF TO FIND OUT WHO OR WHAT LIVED THERE, WHILE THE OTHERS SLEPT ON THE SOFT, WHITE SANDS.

RETURN BY NIGHTFALL!

HAVE NO FEAR, ODYSSEUS. WE WILL RETURN SOON.

BY THE NEXT MORNING, THE MEN WERE MISSING. ODYSSEUS TOOK A GROUP OF MEN TO LOOK FOR THEM. THEY FOUND THE SAILORS EATING BEAUTIFUL FRUIT.

PUT DOWN THAT FRUIT. IF YOU EAT IT, YOU WILL NEVER WANT TO GO HOME!

THIS **LOTUS** FRUIT IS THE BEST THING I'VE EVER EATEN. ALL I CARE ABOUT IS GETTING MORE.

I WANT TO STAY HERE FOREVER.

ODYSSEUS ORDERED TWO MEN TO GRAB EACH MAN WHO HAD EATEN THE LOTUS FRUIT AND CARRY HIM BACK TO THE SHIPS.

AFTER SOME DAYS OF SAILING, THE MEN CAME TO ANOTHER ISLAND.

ODYSSEUS LED HIS MEN INTO A CAVE. ONCE THEY WERE INSIDE, A ONE-EYED GIANT NAMED POLYPHEMUS SEALED THE OPENING.

THE SHEPHERD WHO OWNS THESE SHEEP MUST BE A GIANT BUT HE WILL NOT HARM US. WE ARE ALL SERVANTS OF ZEUS!

THE SAILORS WERE TRAPPED BUT ODYSSEUS WAS ALREADY FIGURING OUT A WAY TO GET THEM OUT OF IT.

I AM POLYPHEMUS, THE SON OF POSEIDON, WHO IS GOD OF THE SEA AND **RIVAL** OF ZEUS. I EAT GREEKS FOR BREAKFAST, LUNCH, AND DINNER. WHO ARE YOU?

MY NAME IS OUTIS.

IN ANCIENT GREEK, THIS MEANT "NO ONE."

HELP! I'VE BEEN BLINDED!

WHILE POLYPHEMUS SLEPT, THE SAILORS CLIMBED ON TOP OF EACH OTHER'S SHOULDERS AND PUT OUT HIS EYE WITH A SHARP STICK. THEN THEY HID IN THE WOOL OF HIS SHEEP TO ESCAPE WHEN THE FLOCK MOVED INTO THE MEADOW.

WHO DID THIS, POLYPHEMUS?

NO ONE? YOU MUST HAVE HAD AN ACCIDENT.

OUTIS! OUTIS!

7

AS THEY SAILED AWAY, MOURNING THE MEN WHOM POLYPHEMUS HAD EATEN, THE GIANT BEGGED HIS FATHER, POSEIDON, TO DOOM ODYSSEUS.

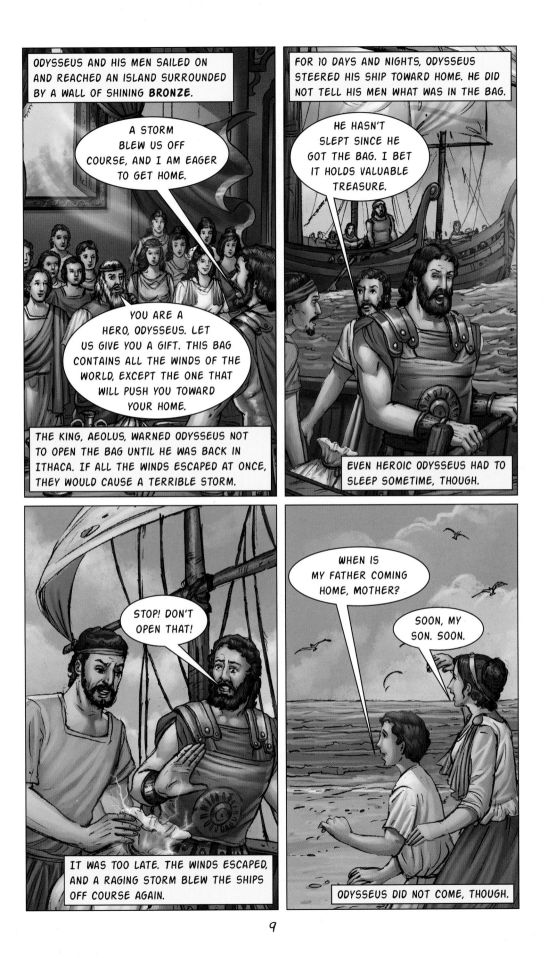

EXHAUSTED AND WEARY FROM THE RAGING STORMS, THE TRAVELERS WERE RELIEVED TO FIND THEMSELVES ON THE SHORES OF ANOTHER ISLAND.

WELCOME! COME UP TO OUR PALACE. WE LOVE TO HAVE PEOPLE FOR SUPPER.

WHAT A TALL GIRL! SHE SEEMS VERY FRIENDLY AND WELCOMING. WE WILL ACCEPT HER OFFER.

THE GIRL HAD SPOKEN THE TRUTH. SHE WAS THE SMALLEST PERSON IN A FAMILY OF GIANTS WHO LOVED TO EAT PEOPLE FOR SUPPER. ONLY 52 OF THE MEN ESCAPED.

THEY SET SAIL AGAIN, LOST AND HEARTBROKEN. SO MANY MEN HAD SURVIVED 10 YEARS OF WAR, ONLY TO BE EATEN BY GREEDY GIANTS. ODYSSEUS SAILED WEST, HOPING TO SEE A FAMILIAR ISLAND THAT WOULD HELP GUIDE HIM HOME.

WHEN THEY ARRIVED AT THE NEXT ISLAND, ODYSSEUS SENT HALF HIS MEN TO EXPLORE. ONE MAN CAME RUNNING BACK WITH A TERRIBLE STORY.

WE MET THE MOST BEAUTIFUL WOMAN I HAVE EVER SEEN. SHE OFFERED US FOOD, BUT I DID NOT EAT. WHEN THE OTHERS ATE, THEY WERE **TRANSFORMED** INTO BEASTS!

ODYSSEUS CALLED HIS MEN TOGETHER AND PREPARED FOR A BATTLE.

YOU CAN'T KILL ME, O MIGHTY ODYSSEUS. I AM IMMORTAL. BESIDES, I LOVE YOU. I HAVE BEEN WAITING FOR YOU . . . FOREVER.

CIRCE PROMISED TO RETURN HIS MEN TO HUMAN FORM IF ODYSSEUS STAYED IN HER PARADISE. ODYSSEUS FINALLY AGREED.

ODYSSEUS SAVED OUR LIVES.

WHAT'S THE HURRY? THIS IS BETTER THAN HOME.

WILL WE GO HOME NOW?

CIRCE DID NOT TURN ODYSSEUS INTO A BEAST, BUT SHE TURNED HIM INTO SOMETHING HE HAD NEVER BEEN BEFORE, A MAN WHO WAS TIRED OF TRAVELING.

AFTER A YEAR ON CIRCE'S ISLAND, ODYSSEUS'S MEN GREW IMPATIENT. THEY TOLD HIM IT WAS TIME TO GO BACK TO ITHACA.

GO IF YOU MUST. BUT WHEN YOU PASS THE ISLAND OF THE SIRENS, YOU MUST NOT LISTEN TO THEIR SINGING. IT WILL DRIVE YOU MAD.

CIRCE GAVE ODYSSEUS WAX FROM HER BEEHIVES, WHICH HE AND HIS MEN COULD USE TO PLUG THEIR EARS.

ODYSSEUS HAD HIS MEN FOLLOW CIRCE'S INSTRUCTIONS. HE ALSO HAD HIS MEN TIE HIM TO THE MAST.

I WANT EVERY MAN TO STUFF HIS EARS WITH BEESWAX. I ALONE WILL HEAR THE BEAUTIFUL SONG OF THE SIRENS.

IT WASN'T LONG BEFORE ODYSSEUS HEARD MUSIC THAT SOUNDED MORE AND MORE BEAUTIFUL.

TAKE THIS SHIP ASHORE! CAN'T YOU HEAR THAT BEAUTIFUL MUSIC? LOOK AT THAT LOVELY ISLAND. I ORDER YOU TO STOP!

WHAT IS HE YELLING ABOUT?

HE MUST BE TELLING US TO ROW FASTER. THAT ISLAND LOOKS SCARY.

AFTER THEY WERE WELL BEYOND THE ISLAND, ODYSSEUS LEARNED THAT THE MAGICAL MUSIC MADE HIM SEE SOMETHING QUITE DIFFERENT FROM WHAT HIS MEN SAW.

THE SIRENS WERE ONLY ONE OF THE DANGERS CIRCE HAD WARNED ODYSSEUS ABOUT. THEY ALSO HAD TO FACE SCYLLA, THE SIX-HEADED SEA MONSTER.

ODYSSEUS DID HIS BEST TO DEFEND HIS SHIP, BUT EACH HEAD ATE ONE OF THE SAILORS. ALL ODYSSEUS HAD TO SHOW FOR HIS EFFORTS WERE SIX MARKS ON HIS SWORD WHERE HE HAD TRIED TO CUT THE MONSTER'S HEADS.

THREE TIMES A DAY, CHARYBDIS, ANOTHER SEA MONSTER, SUCKED EVERYTHING AROUND HER DEEP INTO THE SEA, NEVER TO BE SEEN AGAIN.

ROW, MEN, ROW! IT IS OUR ONLY CHANCE TO ESCAPE THE OCEAN'S POWER.

MIRACULOUSLY, THE BOAT SKIMMED ACROSS THE EDGE OF THE DEADLY WHIRLPOOL.

IN ITHACA, PENELOPE FACED PROBLEMS OF HER OWN. MANY MEN WANTED TO TAKE ODYSSEUS'S PLACE AS HER HUSBAND AND BECOME KING OF ITHACA.

YOU MUST CHOOSE A NEW KING AND HUSBAND.

ODYSSEUS, THE KING, IS ON HIS WAY HOME.

ODYSSEUS IS DEAD, OR HE HAS FOUND ANOTHER WIFE.

MAYBE THESE MEN ARE RIGHT! MAYBE MY FATHER WILL NOT COME HOME.

JUST AS CIRCE HAD WARNED, ODYSSEUS'S MEN WERE PUNISHED FOR EATING THE SUN GOD'S CATTLE. THEIR SHIP WAS SWEPT BACK INTO THE WHIRLPOOL. ONLY ODYSSEUS, WHO DID NOT EAT THE BEEF, SURVIVED.

WHEN ODYSSEUS WOKE UP, HE HEARD LOVELY SINGING. SOFT HANDS BANDAGED HIS WOUNDS AND DRIPPED WATER AND HONEY BETWEEN HIS **PARCHED** LIPS.

WELCOME, ODYSSEUS. YOU AND I ARE THE ONLY PEOPLE ON THIS ISLAND. I'VE BEEN WAITING FOR YOU.

THANK YOU FOR YOUR HELP, KIND LADY. BUT I MUST GET HOME TO ITHACA AND TO MY WIFE AND SON.

BUT CALYPSO INTENDED TO KEEP ODYSSEUS **IMPRISONED** ON HER ISLAND.

WITH NO SHIP OR CREW, ODYSSEUS HAD NO WAY TO ESCAPE CALYPSO.

I LOVE YOU SO MUCH.

MY HEART BELONGS TO PENELOPE. I MUST ESCAPE.

FINALLY, AFTER SEVEN YEARS, CALYPSO ACCEPTED THE TRUTH. ODYSSEUS DID NOT LOVE HER. HE NEVER WOULD.

BACK IN ITHACA, PENELOPE WAITED.

WHEN WILL YOU GIVE US AN ANSWER?

WHEN I FINISH **WEAVING** MY WEDDING VEIL, I WILL TELL YOU WHICH MAN I CHOOSE.

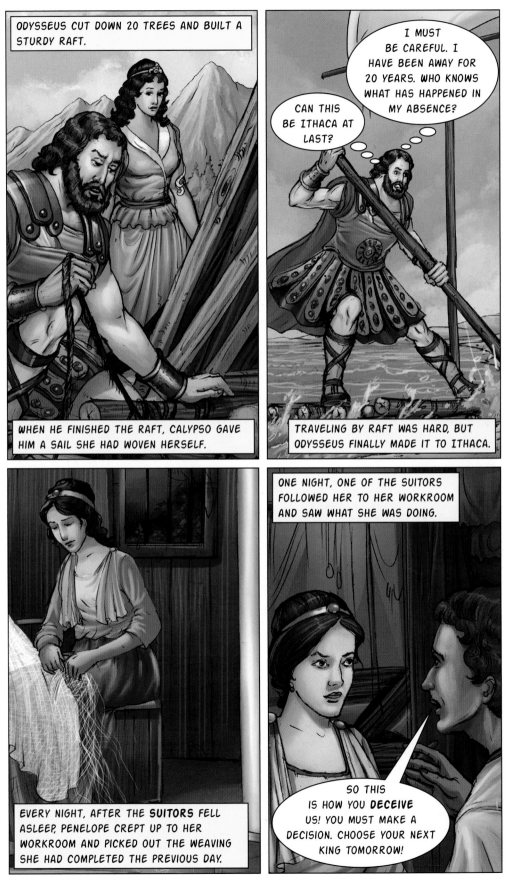

ODYSSEUS CUT DOWN 20 TREES AND BUILT A STURDY RAFT.

WHEN HE FINISHED THE RAFT, CALYPSO GAVE HIM A SAIL SHE HAD WOVEN HERSELF.

I MUST BE CAREFUL. I HAVE BEEN AWAY FOR 20 YEARS. WHO KNOWS WHAT HAS HAPPENED IN MY ABSENCE?

CAN THIS BE ITHACA AT LAST?

TRAVELING BY RAFT WAS HARD, BUT ODYSSEUS FINALLY MADE IT TO ITHACA.

EVERY NIGHT, AFTER THE **SUITORS** FELL ASLEEP, PENELOPE CREPT UP TO HER WORKROOM AND PICKED OUT THE WEAVING SHE HAD COMPLETED THE PREVIOUS DAY.

ONE NIGHT, ONE OF THE SUITORS FOLLOWED HER TO HER WORKROOM AND SAW WHAT SHE WAS DOING.

SO THIS IS HOW YOU **DECEIVE** US! YOU MUST MAKE A DECISION. CHOOSE YOUR NEXT KING TOMORROW!

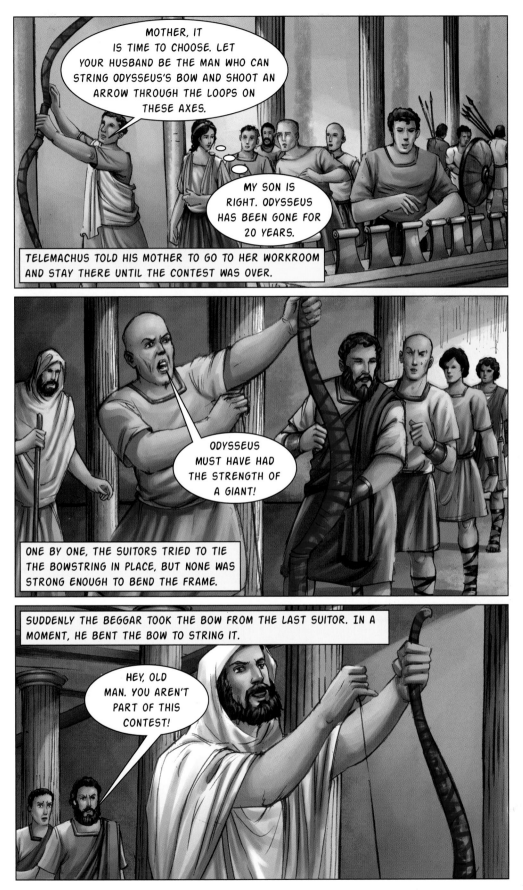

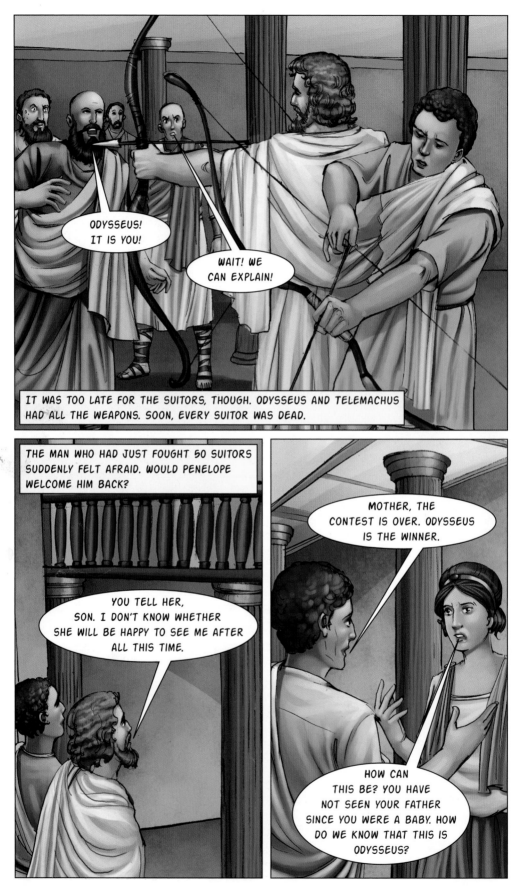

ODYSSEUS! IT IS YOU!

WAIT! WE CAN EXPLAIN!

IT WAS TOO LATE FOR THE SUITORS, THOUGH. ODYSSEUS AND TELEMACHUS HAD ALL THE WEAPONS. SOON, EVERY SUITOR WAS DEAD.

THE MAN WHO HAD JUST FOUGHT 50 SUITORS SUDDENLY FELT AFRAID. WOULD PENELOPE WELCOME HIM BACK?

YOU TELL HER, SON. I DON'T KNOW WHETHER SHE WILL BE HAPPY TO SEE ME AFTER ALL THIS TIME.

MOTHER, THE CONTEST IS OVER. ODYSSEUS IS THE WINNER.

HOW CAN THIS BE? YOU HAVE NOT SEEN YOUR FATHER SINCE YOU WERE A BABY. HOW DO WE KNOW THAT THIS IS ODYSSEUS?

PENELOPE KNEW A SECRET. SHE PLANNED TO TEST THIS MAN TO FIND OUT IF HE REALLY WAS HER HUSBAND.

MY LORD, I WILL TELL THE SERVANTS TO MOVE THE BED YOU MADE US INTO ANOTHER ROOM.

VERY WELL. BUT HOW WILL YOUR SERVANTS MOVE THE BED SINCE I CARVED IT OUT OF THE CROWN OF THE TREE THAT GROWS IN THE CENTER OF THE PALACE? ITS ROOTS ARE DEEP IN THE GROUND.

ODYSSEUS KNEW THE SECRET! NOW PENELOPE KNEW THAT HER HUSBAND HAD COME HOME AT LAST.

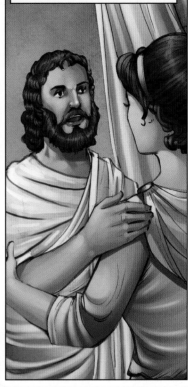

AND THAT WAS THE STORY THAT HOMER, THE BLIND POET, TOLD THOUSANDS OF YEARS AGO. IT IS A STORY THAT PEOPLE STILL READ TODAY.

THUS ENDS MY TALE OF THE HERO WHO WON THE WAR AND THE HARDSHIPS AND SORROWS HE SUFFERED TO RETURN TO HIS HOME AND THOSE HE LOVED, HIS SON, TELEMACHUS, AND HIS WIFE, PENELOPE.

The Story of Odysseus

According to the stories written about Odysseus, he traveled to many strange and fantastic places along his voyage. People often wonder if these places were real and if so, where they would be located. Some ancient historians, such as Herodotus and Thucydides, pass on different versions of myths related to the travels of Odysseus. Eratosthenes and Apollonius of Rhodes, headmasters at the ancient library at Alexandria during the third century BC, believed the locations were made up. The first century Greek geographer Strabo took another approach. He believed that many locations from the story were connected with real places, even if some of the details given by Homer might not be entirely accurate. Scholars continue to debate the question even to this day.

The Voyage of Odysseus

Island of Circe

Italy

Sirens

Ithaca – Odysseus's home

Thrace

Straits of Scylla and Charybdis

Man-Eating Lystragonians

Greece

Aegean Sea

Troy

Anatolia

Aeolus

Thrinacia – home of Helios

Land of the Cyclopes

Crete

Island of Calypso

Mediterranean Sea

Land of the Lotus Eaters

Egypt

Odysseus's Journey

Glossary

bronze (BRONZ) A golden brown blend of copper and tin metals.

deceive (dih-SEEV) To mislead or to make someone believe something that is not true.

heroes (HEER-ohz) People who are brave and have noble characters.

hound (HOWND) To make repeated demands or to pressure someone to do something.

imprisoned (im-PRIZ-und) Confined or kept in a certain place, like a prison.

lotus (LOH-tus) A plant that has yellow flowers and seeds and leaves that can be eaten and that grows in the water.

mortals (MOR-tulz) Human beings.

muse (MYOOZ) A source of inspiration.

nymph (NIMF) A beautiful maiden who lived in the forests, trees, and water in Greek stories.

parched (PAHRCHD) Dried out.

rabble (RA-bel) A large, disorganized group of noisy people who are hard to control.

rival (RY-vul) Someone who tries to beat someone else at something.

suitors (SOO-turz) Men who seek to marry a woman.

swineherd (SWYN-herd) A person who takes care of pigs.

transformative (tranz-FOR-muh-tiv) Something that can cause another thing to be changed.

transformed (tranz-FORMD) Changed shape or appearance.

weaving (WEE-ving) Lacing strands of thread together to make cloth.

wrath (RATH) Extreme anger or punishment for a crime.

Index

Websites

Due to the changing nature of Internet links, PowerKids Press has developed an online list of websites related to the subject of this book. This site is updated regularly. Please use this link to access the list:

www.powerkidslinks.com/grmy/voyage